SAVING
MY MONEY

Published in paperback in 2015 by Wayland

Senior editor: Camilla Lloyd
Designer: Paul Cherrill
Digital Colour: Carl Gordon

10 9 8 7 6 5 4 3 2 1

Dewey Number: 332'.024-dc22
ISBN: 978 0 7502 8920 7

Wayland, an imprint of Hachette Children's Group
Part of Hodder & Stoughton
Carmelite House, 50 Victoria Embankment
London EC4Y 0DZ

British Library Cataloguing in Publication Data:
Llewellyn, Claire.
    Saving my money. -- (Your money!)
    1. Money--Juvenile literature. 2. Finance, Personal--
    Juvenile literature. 3. Saving and investment--
    Juvenile literature.
    I. Title II. Series III. Gordon, Mike, 1948 Mar. 16-

Printed in China

An Hachette UK Company
www.hachette.co.uk
www.hachettechildrens.co.uk

SAVING
MY MONEY

Written by
Claire Llewellyn

Illustrated by
Mike Gordon

WAYLAND

Have you ever seen something you really want but don't have the money to buy?

You could ask Mum or Dad for it...

...or you could save up and buy it yourself.

Saving means putting money aside so that you can use it in the future.

If you save money steadily, then your savings will grow and grow — just like tiny seeds.

So how do
you start saving
money?

Every time you get
some money, don't
spend all of it...

...put half of it in your money box
and keep it somewhere safe.

Saving can be tricky at times.
It's very tempting to spend your money...

...and there are so many fun things to buy.

But if you keep saving, not spending,
your money, then week by week,
your savings will grow.

Before you know it, you'll reach your goal.

Grown-ups need to save money, too.
Saving helps them to plan for the future...

...to pay for things that cost a lot.

When you are saving a lot of money, it's best to have a savings account in a post office or a bank.

Your money will earn interest. This means that a little extra money is added to your savings, helping them to grow even more!

In the future, you can use your savings
to buy something extra special...

...or do something you really want to do.

Saving money is a good habit.
What would you like to do in the future?

What could you save for?

Notes For Parents and Teachers

We all need to be able to manage our money and make financial decisions. The four books in the 'Your Money' series are intended as a first step along this path. Based on children's everyday lives, the series is a light-hearted introduction to money, everyday financial transactions, planning and saving and financial choices.

'Saving my Money' explains how, by spending sensibly, children can save some of their money. It discusses how saving helps us to plan for the future and enables us to buy or do the things we want. It looks at the best places to save money and introduces the concept of earning interest in a savings account.

Suggested follow-up activities

- Devise a Ludo-type game with your children to be played with dice. Think of examples of getting money, spending money and saving money. For example, 'You get your pocket money today, move forward 2 squares'; or 'You lose 50p. Move back 3 squares.'

- Make a collection of different types of moneybox. Which one does the job best? Why? Which one is the children's favourite? Why? Now ask the children to design a moneybox of their own. Make sure it's easier to put money in than take it out!

- Imagine you are going to buy a pet. Come up with a list of questions you would have to ask.

E.g. what would the pet cost to buy; what essential equipment would the pet need; what other costs might be necessary? Then take the children to a pet shop and find the answers to your questions.

• Take your children inside a bank so that they can see what happens there. You could open a savings account for them and suggest they save some of their money.

• Ask children to think of one thing they would really like to buy and one thing they would really like to do. Help them to find out how much it would cost. If they saved £1 a week, how long would they take to buy it? Can they think of any ways they could get or earn the money?

• What things do adults need to save for? What are the most expensive things that they are likely to need or want? Ask children for suggestions or give them picture clues.

• Get children to draw a picture of something they dream of doing in the future. Get them to write a caption – e.g. 'One day, I want to ride a camel in the desert.'

BOOKS TO READ

'Learning About Money: Saving Money' by Mary Firestone
(First Fact Books, 2004)
'Using Money' by Rebecca Rissman
(Heinemann Library, 2010)

USEFUL WEBSITES

www.pfeg.org
www.mymoneyonline.org

INDEX